Joy Boosters

120 Ways
to Encourage Older Adults

MISSY BUCHANAN

UPPER ROOM BOOKS®
NASHVILLE

The Upper Room® website http://www.upperroom.org

UPPER ROOM®, UPPER ROOM BOOKS®, and design logos are trademarks owned by The Upper Room®, A Ministry of GBOD®, Nashville, Tennessee. All rights reserved.

Cover design: Marc Whitaker / www.mtwdesign.net
Interior design: PerfecType, Nashville, TN

Library of Congress Cataloging-in-Publication Data

Buchanan, Missy.
  Joy boosters : encouragement for older adults / by Missy Buchanan.
      p. cm.
  ISBN 978-0-8358-1192-7 (print)—ISBN 978-0-8358-1193-4 (mobi)—ISBN 978-0-8358-1194-1 (epub)
  1. Church work with older people. 2. Older people—Psychology. 3. Encouragement. 4. Older people—Religious life. I. Title.
  BV4435.B83 2013
  259'.3—dc23
                                    2012035613

Printed in the United States of America

I dedicate this book to my sister and brother,
Martha McGlothlin and John McGlothlin Jr.,
who so generously loved our parents
and made every effort to bring joy
into their lives.

CONTENTS

INTRODUCTION

Older adults who struggle with physical limitations and the losses that inevitably come with aging may experience life as barren and dry. As a family member or church leader, you want to encourage senior adults; but perhaps you don't know what to do. How do you put a smile on the face of a frail man who is slumped over in a wheelchair? What can you do to cheer a grandmother who has just moved to an assisted living facility? How can you encourage an elderly man whose wife must now live in a memory care facility?

Joy Boosters is a response to those questions. Designed much like a pocket guide, *Joy Boosters* is a book of ideas that will help you become more confident in your efforts to encourage older adults on their spiritual walk. Each chapter is filled with suggestions that will bring joy to an older adult. Some ideas are geared toward church participation, while others target actions family members can take. All may be adapted by both church and family to meet the needs of older adults.

Connecting through Questions and Conversation

Older adults offer a valuable link to the past, and questions that invite conversation are the doorway. Use the open-ended questions below to prompt meaningful discussion. Some questions are lighthearted and fun; others are more intense and thought-provoking. Select questions that seem appropriate for each individual and situation.

- In what city or town were you born?

- What was the funniest thing you or your sibling did as a child?

- What was the name of one of your favorite childhood friends? What did you enjoy doing together?

- Did you have a nickname? What was it? Who gave it to you? How did you feel about it?

Dot
Squirt

- How did you get to and from school as a child? as a teenager?

- What was your favorite subject in school? Least favorite? Why?

- What was a typical summer day like when you were a child?

- What was your first paid job? What were your responsibilities?

- How did you learn to drive? Who taught you? What did you drive?

- What memories do you have of going to church as a child? as a teenager? as an adult?

- When was your first trip away from home?

- How did you and your spouse first meet?

- Of what achievement are you the most proud?

- If you could go back in time to a certain day in your life, what day would you choose?

- Looking back on your life, where can you see the hand of God most clearly evidenced?

- What would you consider to be the best year of your life?

- What loss or failure later turned into unexpected joy?

- What is something you have always longed to do but have never done?

- Who is someone you greatly admire? Why?

◆ If you had no physical or financial limitations, where would you like to travel?

◆ What do you miss most about being young?

◆ What is the best part of growing old?

◆ What advice can you share with younger generations?

◆ For what are you most thankful?

Keeping the Faith

The church plays a vital role in the lives of older adults. Keeping seniors who face physical or mental decline connected to a faith community should be a church priority. Adapt these ideas to meet the needs of older adults in your church community.

◆ **Mission trip memory.** Provide an older adult with the itinerary of a youth group's mission trip and ask him to pray for the group each day. Have the youth make and laminate a sign with the older person's name or photo. Make the sign large enough to be visible in a group photo but small enough for easy transport. At stops along the journey, gather the youth and adult leaders together for a group photo and ask one of the youth to hold the sign. Snap a photo, and record a brief description of the location. Be sure to include photos

Tips for those visiting from churches

Don't just pop in for a visit. Generally, it is best to contact an older adult to determine the best time to visit. If she is easily confused, call a family member instead. Keep in mind that many older adults have schedules for caregivers and therapists. Having a set time to visit also helps those with hearing loss who may not hear a doorbell or a knock on the door. For many older adults, Sunday afternoon is a good time to visit since there are fewer conflicts with medical appointments and social events.

Wear an easy-to-read name tag with the church logo clearly visible. Even older adults who have been longtime church members will appreciate not having the pressure of recalling a visitor's name. Wearing name tags can also be a subtle evangelistic tool. As others in a retirement community notice your name tag, they will identify you with a specific church family.

Leave an oversized card announcing who came to visit. Older adults will enjoy displaying a special calling card that tells when church members came to visit. Family members will also appreciate knowing that church members have been by to visit their loved one. Since business cards are small and difficult to read for aging eyes, it is best to use larger cards. Add a personal note, and put it in a visible place before you leave.

of the actual mission project. Send photos and descriptions to the older adult at different intervals during the trip so that he can enjoy receiving multiple mailings. Or wait until you return and assemble the photos into an album. Be sure to acknowledge his prayer support for the mission project.

◆ **More than a dress rehearsal.** Ask older adults who live in a local retirement community to be the audience for the dress rehearsal of a children's musical production at church. Seniors will love watching the costumed youngsters perform in a less-crowded venue than the actual performance. Several months in advance, contact the activity director of the retirement community to coordinate transportation and other details. Arrange for church volunteers to greet the residents and assist them safely to their seats. Following the performance, host a brief reception allowing the children an opportunity to interact with the older adults.

◆ **Lenten or Advent devotional booklets.** Invite older adults to write for a Lenten or Advent devotional booklet. For those who have difficulty with handwriting or computer skills, offer to be a personal scribe. These devotional booklets can be given as a gift to the congregation. Whenever possible, create opportunities to encourage older adults to share their faith journey with others.

◆ **Church dinners.** Does your church have a midweek dinner or occasional potluck? Older adults who are unable to participate in these fellowship meals will enjoy a take-out container of food from the event. Sunday school classes, Bible study groups, and other small groups can also make individual containers of homemade soup to deliver to older adults. Be sure to include a note of encouragement and a scripture verse.

◆ **Share the bounty.** Appeal to gardeners in the congregation to share their bounty with older congregants who no longer tend a garden. A basket of homegrown produce will put a smile on the face of most any older adult. Who can resist tree-ripened peaches or a just-picked tomato?

◆ **Photo gallery.** Honor the seniors in your church by creating an art gallery of current photographs of the older adults. Refrain from using typical church directory photos. Instead ask volunteer photographers to visit the seniors and photograph the older persons holding an object that is especially dear to them. Ask them to share the story about the special object. Display the photographs and the stories at your church. Make the photo gallery available for several weeks. Invite the congregation to stroll through and read about their elders in faith.

◆ **Newsletter highlight.** Regularly profile a homebound senior in the church newsletter. Include information about past church involvement, family, and special interests. With permission, include a mailing address and encourage members to send cards and letters. If privacy is a concern, ask members to send cards to the church office to be delivered to the older adult.

- **Christian resource library.** Check with area retirement communities about your congregation donating a collection of Christian reading materials appropriate for older adults. Inside each book or magazine, place a permanent bookplate containing the church's contact information along with an invitation to call the church if the older adults have questions or concerns. You may also provide bookmarks with the church's name and logo for residents to keep. Remember that many unchurched older adults have spiritual questions. Use the resource library as an outreach opportunity.

- **Helping older adults to serve others.** Sometimes older adults have difficulty imagining how they can serve others when they feel limited in what they can do physically. Oftentimes, they just need a little encouragement and a few supplies. For the older man who loves to raise houseplants, supply him with pots and potting soil so that he can take cuttings from his own plants to share with neighbors. For the woman who loves to knit or crochet, provide her with yarn to make a blanket for every baby born in her church or for a local women's shelter. For the older adult who enjoys writing poetry, invite her to write a booklet of poems that could be sold at a church fund-raiser to support mission projects.

◆ **Church directory.** When your church updates its pictorial directory, don't overlook older adults who are unable to come to the church to have their photo taken. Send your church photographer to the homes of older adults to take a current photo. Be sure to update their contact information as well. Putting older adults in your church's directory keeps them visible to the congregation.

◆ **Prayer.** Pass prayer requests from older adults to your church's prayer team or pastors. Also, provide the seniors with a copy of the church's most recent prayer list and invite them to pray for those listed.

◆ **Senior nativity.** Encourage older adults at retirement communities to step into the Christmas story. Organize a nativity in which all of the characters, from wise men to angels, are played by older adults. Borrow or make costumes. Keep costumes simple for those who require canes, walkers, or wheelchairs. Ask a church member to read the nativity story so that no memorization is required for the older adults. Volunteers dressed in black as stagehands can assist by pushing wheelchairs as needed. Invite an ensemble from the church choir to provide Christmas music for a sing-along at the conclusion of the presentation.

◆ **Adopt-a-Senior.** Invite families, Sunday school classes, and Bible study groups to adopt an older adult who can no longer attend church. Ask the group to commit to making phone calls or mailing letters in addition to a monthly face-to-face visit with the older adult. Encourage the group to build relationships with the senior adults, even occasionally going out to eat or having a picnic together.

- **Communion.** As a visual reminder of a church's homebound members, it is helpful to display the bags that will later be taken to serve Communion to home-bound members. Place the bags either on the altar or at the foot of the altar. Ask the minister to remind the congregation that visitation teams will be serving the consecrated Communion elements to those unable to come to church.

- **VBS for older adults.** Vacation Bible school is not just for kids! Older adults will also enjoy a special weeklong event planned in their honor. Create a theme especially for seniors, perhaps focusing on older characters of the Bible. Plan a two-hour schedule that moves older adults through a series of activities and classes including music, Bible study, and refreshments. Involve church members of all ages as teachers and helpers. Host the event at a retirement community or at a church with transportation provided.

Transitioning to a New Home

Older adults are not exempt from the fear and uncertainty that come with moving to a new place. Many struggle with leaving behind a home where they've created so many memories. Trying to decide what to take, what to sell, and what to give away can be overwhelming. Even finding their way around a new home at a retirement center can be confusing. Use these suggestions to help make the transition easier for an older adult.

◆ **Blessing the home.** Ask your minister to preside over a "Bless This New Home" service for an older loved one. Invite a small number of friends and family to attend an intimate worship service at her new residence. Sing hymns, read scripture, offer a prayer and a message about new beginnings. A service of blessing will help set a positive tone for your loved one's transition.

◆ **Personalized change-of-address cards.** Take a photo of an older loved one in front of his new residence. Use it to create personalized change-of-address cards for friends and family. Include a note encouraging friends and family to send cards and letters. Your loved one will take pleasure in receiving a bounty of mail at his new address.

◆ **Hometown newspaper.** If an aging loved one is moving from a town where she has lived for many years, have her hometown newspaper delivered to her new residence. She will look forward to reading about life in the town she left behind.

◆ **Videotaped walk-through of home.** Before an older loved one moves from her longtime home, film a walking tour through every room. Don't forget the exterior and the backyard. Narrate interesting details and highlight uplifting memories of what life was like in that house. Ask the older adult to make comments too. Make a DVD from the video so the older adult can watch it again and again and share it with new friends.

◆ **Handheld cross.** When an older adult moves to a new home, she may find comfort in holding a small wooden cross that fits into the palm of her hand. The handheld cross serves as a visible and tactile reminder that God is always with her. They are available at many Christian book stores and online.

◆ **Family poster.** Have a favorite family photo enlarged into a wall poster for a loved one's new residence.

Using a marker, write the first name of each person on the photo in easy-to-read letters. The poster will serve as a conversation starter as staff members and others drop by.

Encouraging from a Distance

Caring for an aging loved one who lives far away can be frustrating and stressful for both the family members and the older adult. However, there are things that will help encourage a senior even when miles separate you.

◆ **Pocket prayers.** Create a set of pocket-sized cards with brief prayers written by family members or friends. A grandchild might write the following:

Dear God, help my Gramps know how much I love and miss him. Let him feel my hug even though we are miles away. In Christ's name I pray. Amen.

Invite young family members to decorate the blank side of each card, then laminate the cards to keep them from becoming worn. Just knowing that family members are praying for him will boost an older loved one's mood.

♦ **Find a companion.** Contact the church in a loved one's community. Ask for recommendations for a volunteer or a person you can hire to spend a few hours each week with your older loved one as a companion. Communicate regularly with this person so that she can act as a surrogate family member, doing activities that you would pursue with your loved one if you were there. Remember, background checks and references are important.

♦ **Write a letter.** It may seem old-fashioned in a world of electronic communication, but a handwritten letter is a treasure for older adults. Get in the habit of writing a weekly letter to an older loved one. Most seniors take great pleasure in reading and rereading a letter; they will even share it with friends!

♦ **"Remember When" scrapbook.** Don't wait for a funeral to collect memories about an aging loved one. Ask family and friends to send you their funny or heartfelt remembrances. Create a "Remember When" scrapbook to provide him hours of comfort when you are apart.

♦ **Door and window decorations.** Have someone decorate the front door or window of an older loved one's residence to reflect each season and upcoming holiday. She will anticipate the festive, ever-changing decorations without the worry of having to do it herself.

◆ **Family heirloom photographs.** If an older loved one has given you a special heirloom or item from her belongings, take a photo to show how you are using it in your own home. For example, let her see family and friends enjoying a meal served on the dishes she gave you. Snap a picture of her mother's old armoire now in your guest bedroom. Help her visualize how you are enjoying the things she has passed on to you.

Using Photographs to Create Smiles

People often say that the item they would most likely rescue from a burning house would be their collection of photographs. It's not surprising that older adults wholeheartedly agree. Photographs reconnect them to the stories of their past. These creative photo projects will bring joy to older adults.

◆ **Photo placemats.** Older adults will enjoy personalized placemats made from copies of their old photographs. Create a collage of selected photos or enlarge a single photo to fit placemat-sized (11-by-17) paper. Use a color copier to make duplicate copies, then laminate them for easy maintenance. Placemats can be used daily by an aging loved one or during family celebrations.

◆ **A pictorial epitaph.** Invite an older adult to reflect on her life by sorting through her collection of old photographs. Ask her to select ten photographs that represent how she would like to be remembered long after she is gone. She might choose photographs that include her favorite lifetime roles: a caring mother and grandmother, a travel partner and friend to her husband, a school teacher, a member of the church choir. Make copies of the photos so that the originals can be preserved. Use them to create a photo collage for her wall or bedside as a daily reminder of the impact of her life.

◆ **Older adults as photographers.** Borrow an idea from brides who place disposable cameras on reception tables so that guests can capture impromptu moments. If your loved one lives in a retirement community, supply him with a disposable camera to pass around to neighbors and friends at mealtime or during a special event. Props like oversized sunglasses and feather boas can add to the fun. Have someone available to help operate the camera if needed. Make copies of the photos to share with the older adults. Or create a special bulletin board to display the photos for all to enjoy.

◆ **Trip down memory lane.** Some older adults are unable to travel long distances because of physical limitations. But with some creative planning, you can take an older adult on a "photo trip" to see significant places from his past. Think of places that have strong emotional ties to him. Take current photos of these locations, which might include his family's farm, the downtown of the city where he grew up, or the business where he had his first job.

◆ **Photo wreath.** For a space-saving way to display photographs, create a door wreath from an older adult's collection of photos. Purchase a flat wooden wreath from a craft store, or cut a shape from foam board. Glue copies of photographs printed on cardstock onto the wreath form, overlapping as needed to create a circular collage. Hang the photo wreath at the older person's residence.

◆ **Personalized playing cards.** If an older loved one enjoys playing card games, she will love showing off a deck of personalized photo cards made from a favorite family photo or perhaps a picture from her youth. Photo cards are available through many online sites and at most photo shops.

◆ **Create a photo book.** Don't wait to celebrate an older adult's life. Use an online service or photo store to create a personalized hardback photo book about his life while he can still savor each page. Capture the highlights of his many years through words and images.

◆ **Organize old photos.** Volunteer to help an older person sort through boxes of old photographs. Label each photo with names, place, and time so that future generations can more fully appreciate their heritage. If possible, also scan and save the photos digitally.

◆ **Old 8mm movies.** Many older adults own reels of 8mm movie film. Preserve these memories by transferring the film to a digital format. Then roll out the red carpet, and host a premiere of the film at a special family gathering. Your loved one can offer commentary on the people and places in the movie.

Planning Mini-Getaways

Many older adults feel uncomfortable with long trips that take them away from their routines and familiar surroundings. Yet short outings can be the perfect pick-me-up for older adults who long for a day away. Plan a personalized mini-trip and give an older adult a real boost.

◆ **Seasonal sights.** Help an older adult anticipate each new season of the year. In spring, make a date to take her to see the azaleas, dogwoods, or cherry blossoms. On a warm summer day, go for a drive to get an ice-cold lemonade or an ice cream sundae. When fall arrives, take a trip to a pumpkin patch or to see the changing leaves. Even a cold winter evening becomes bright with an outing to see Christmas lights and decorations. Be intentional about creating a seasonal respite from a loved one's daily routine. She will look

Tips for traveling with older adults

Before heading out, consider these important tips for making a day trip more enjoyable for older loved ones.

Be sensitive to the physical limitations. Getting in and out of a vehicle is especially difficult for many older adults with arthritis. Often trucks or large sport utility vehicles are too high for them to get in comfortably. Also, some cars are so low to the ground that they are difficult as well. Minivans or small SUVs often work best for those who struggle with arthritic pain or a lack of strength. If you don't own one, consider asking a friend or family member if you can borrow a vehicle for the day.

Allow plenty of time. It takes time to load and unload wheelchairs and walkers. Older adults with physical

---

forward to each seasonal outing and will savor the memories long after it is over.

◆ **Picnic or private dining.** Many older adults feel pressured at busy restaurants—they worry about spilling food, eating too slowly, or not being able to hear because of background noise. If those worries are true for your aging loved one, create a private dining experience instead. A picnic lunch at a local park or lunch limitations may also need help with seat belts. Don't try to hurry them along. Just plan extra time in your schedule.

Rent a handicap van. If an older loved one uses a wheelchair or power chair, consider renting a handicap van with ramp access. The older person can remain securely in his chair during transport. Many services even rent these vans by the hour, which can make trips to the doctor and other short outings more comfortable for your loved one and more convenient for you.

Know your destination. When possible, scope out your final destination and know where the handicap parking and restrooms are located. This simple act can save time and frustration.

for two on your patio may be just the change of venue that will make a dining experience most enjoyable.

♦ **Hot air balloon festival.** Towns and cities across the country host hot air balloon festivals. If one is coming to your area, see when the balloons will lift off. Find a convenient place to watch the vibrant display of color as the balloons take to the air. Bring comfortable, portable seating too. It will be an experience an older loved one will never forget.

- **Personal chauffeur.** Many older adults grieve when longtime friends move away, even if it is just across town. Those unable to drive themselves fear that they will be unable to see their friends again face-to-face. Don't wait for an older loved one to ask you to drive them to visit friends who have moved away. Let her know you will be her chauffeur for the day! Choose a time that works for both parties and watch the joy that comes as old friends reconnect.

- **Living history farm.** Many areas of the country have living farms that preserve the history of the region. Usually these are actual working farms that present life as it used to be. Most have gardens and animals, along with volunteers who fulfill the daily tasks of life on a farm. For older adults who grew up on a farm, this outing provides a delightful opportunity to reminisce about life as they recall it.

Making Music
for Older Ears

Music has a unique way of lifting the spirits of older adults. Watch their faces light up when they hear favorite tunes of their youth. Adapt the following suggestions for either individual or group use.

◆ **Name that hymn.** Many older adults remember the words to hymns long after other memories have faded. In fact, hymns have a way of buoying weary spirits. Gather a collection of hymns on CDs, including both choral and instrumental versions. Make an impromptu game by playing part of a selection, then asking an older loved one to name the hymn or sing the next line.

◆ **Big band.** The big band sounds of Tommy Dorsey and Glenn Miller will likely elicit a strong nostalgic response from an older loved one. Spend an afternoon together just listening to CDs of big band music.

Listening to songs will likely lead to your loved one sharing stories and memories.

◆ **Rhythm instruments.** Gather a variety of rhythm instruments. Check with area schools and churches for tambourines, maracas, bongo drums, rhythm sticks, castanets, sand blocks, tom-toms, and more. For a brain-boosting activity, invite older adults to copy a brief rhythm pattern that you play for them. Or put on some lively music, and invite everybody to improvise with instruments.

◆ **Jazz it up!** Many high schools now have their own jazz bands or ensembles. Check with the local band director about the possibility of a mini-jazz concert for a group of older adults. When the band strikes up a familiar tune, watch the toes start tapping!

◆ **Never too old for lessons.** Older adults need to know that it's not too late to learn how to play a musical instrument. Even those who think they have no musical talent will have fun learning to stroke a ukulele or an autoharp. Be resourceful. Look around the community for people who would be willing to teach an older adult how to play a musical instrument.

◆ **Kazoo band.** There's something fun about the buzzing sound of a kazoo. Older adults will enjoy kazooing together as a group. Choose an upbeat tune that everyone knows, then have some impromptu kazoo fun!

◆ **Hand dance.** Hand dancing is not only enjoyable, it is good exercise for arthritic hands. Select a familiar song or hymn and create gentle hand motions to accompany each line. Teach the choreography to the older adults. Invite them to perform their hand dance at an upcoming event.

- **Bluegrass jam.** Older adults are drawn to the pure sounds of bluegrass music known for the fiddle, banjo, and guitar. Extend an invitation to a local bluegrass band to play for a group of seniors.

- **Children's choir.** Who can resist the angelic voices of children? Check with the director of a children's choir at your church or local elementary school about presenting a concert for older adults. Don't wait for the Christmas rush!

- **Senior gospel choir.** Being a member of a senior gospel choir invigorates many older adults who still enjoy singing. If you need a director, your church's music director can suggest potential volunteers. Ask the seniors to share the names of their favorite gospel tunes. Try to include as many as possible in the song repertoire. Encourage the group to sing at church events or at retirement communities.

- **Karaoke.** Many older adults may not be familiar with a karaoke machine, but once they are introduced, they will get a kick out of a sing-along session! Select songs that most seniors know, then invite them to pass around the microphone, and join in the fun.

- **Personal recital.** Ask a child or teenager to give a personal recital for an older loved one in her home. A recital is good practice for someone who is learning to play the piano or another instrument. And don't forget those taking dance or voice lessons. Older adults will delight in their own private recital.

Encouraging Hobbies and Interests

For many older adults, it may seem that aging has put an end to enjoying their favorite hobbies and interests. The frail great-grandfather who used to spend hours in the garden can no longer bend over to pull weeds or plant seeds. The older woman who had once been a talented seamstress now cannot see well enough to thread the needle.

In spite of physical limitations that come with age, you can help older adults find ways to modify their favorite hobbies and explore new ones! But don't make the mistake of thinking that hobbies are just a way for seniors to pass the time mindlessly. Creativity is life-affirming! Help them rekindle interests that will boost their self-esteem and give them purpose.

◆ **Publications with a purpose.** Nurture the interest of an older adult by subscribing to a publication that focuses on a favorite pastime. From antique collecting to miniature trains, from sports to travel, there's a publication for almost every interest that will encourage older adults to keep learning.

◆ **Library outing.** Schedule a monthly trip to the local library to keep an older adult well-stocked with books. Older adults may be intimidated by the size, scope, and technology of the library system. However, you can offer to be a personal escort, teaching an older adult how to utilize the library's assets. Be sure to ask about book options in large print for those who can no longer read small type.

◆ **Book club.** If an older loved one is an avid reader, encourage her to start a book club among her peers. Provide the organizational support she needs to make it successful. Help her decide on a favorite book and questions to discuss. Remember too that older adults often enjoy rereading books of their youth. Make flyers with time and place for each club meeting. Offer to help others get copies of the book.

◆ **Bird-watching.** Aging can bring a new opportunity to spend time in quiet pursuit of our feathered friends. Even older adults who have never shown an interest in bird-watching may get excited as they scan the trees and skies, looking for markings on birds to identify a certain species. Provide binoculars and books on how to identify birds.

◆ **Mini-gardening.** Terrariums, bonsai trees, potted plants, and windowsill herb gardens are ways for an older gardener to continue his hobby long after he can maintain a larger outdoor garden. Raised gardening beds also offer a great opportunity for him to get back to nature.

◆ **Current events.** Keeping pace with what is going on in the world helps older adults to be mentally involved in life. Invite discussion of current events. Use a world map to locate unfamiliar places in the news. Remember also to look for stories with a positive message to balance the amount of negative news.

◆ **Fishing.** For older adults who no longer have the physical stamina to unload a boat or haul the supplies necessary for a fishing trip, arrange a morning at a local lake or private pond. Ask family or church members who are sportsmen to provide basic fishing equipment and assist the older adults in their pursuit of the biggest fish!

◆ **Prayer beads.** Making prayer beads from colorful beads, baubles, and stones will delight many older adults who are interested in prayer and meditation. Check with a local church to find someone who can teach the older adults how to make prayer beads. You can also find instructions to make prayer beads online. Distribute the finished prayer beads to hospitals or mission ministries.

◆ **Travel festival.** Most older adults have experienced the joy of travel to places near or far. Help recreate those special memories by hosting a travel festival. Encourage seniors to bring stories, photos, and souvenirs from a favorite trip they've taken in the past. It's a fun way to celebrate their memories of favorite destinations and to spark conversation.

◆ **Sewing and needlework.** Older adults sometimes worry that needlework hobbies are becoming a lost art. Organize a sewing circle that includes people of all ages who come together to quilt, crochet, embroider, or knit. Specialty magnifying glasses and large-eye needles can help those with vision problems. Honor the older adults by displaying their finished pieces.

◆ **Recycle and renew.** Ask people to donate their old greeting cards for a project that will give purpose to older adults. Provide card-making supplies including scissors, glue, markers, card stock, and envelopes. Invite the seniors to create new cards from the old, even scripting new verses for all occasions. Package several cards together and tie with ribbon. Donations for the cards can help fund a ministry effort at church or within the retirement community. It's also an affordable way for seniors to give cards to each other.

Finding Laughter

A sense of humor is vital to the well-being of older adults. Sometimes all they need is a jump-start to laughter. You can help an older adult find the brighter side of aging, even when days seem dark, by using and adapting these suggestions.

- **Happy thoughts flip book.** Create a personalized book of happy thoughts for an older loved one. Write inspirational thoughts, quotes, or jokes in easy-to-read print on four-by-six index cards. Use spiral-bound note cards or place the index cards in a photo album for easy flipping. The book of happy thoughts will lift the spirits of older adults on an ordinary day.

- **Funny church signs and bulletin bloopers.** Put a little holy humor into an older adult's routine. Gather funny sayings from church signs and bloopers from church bulletins. Write them in a notebook, and invite him to share the funny sayings with his friends.

◆ **Story prompts.** Sometimes older adults just need a prompt to recall a funny story from their past.

What's something funny that happened at your wedding? Tell a funny story about something you did as a child. Tell something funny that once happened at church.

In a group setting, one person's story will likely trigger another's story. Providing a question is an easy way to get the laughter ball rolling among older adults.

◆ **Preschool parade.** Check your church's preschool program for special events in which the children dress in costumes. Maybe it is a Fall Festival, Western Day, or Mardi Gras. Work with the preschool director to coordinate a parade in which the children walk through the common area of a senior care facility. Watching the costumed youngsters will delight the older adults.

◆ **Joke of the week.** Surprise an older loved one with a weekly chuckle. Each week, print an appropriate joke on a postcard and drop it in the mail. Your loved one will enjoy receiving the laugh and enjoy receiving mail. Chances are, he will also share the jokes with others.

◆ **Old TV shows on DVD.** Rent or borrow DVDs of light-hearted television shows from the past. There are old Andy Williams' specials, reruns of Lawrence Welk, Bing Crosby, and Bob Hope, too. Help an older loved queue up the DVD and enjoy reminiscing together.

Celebrating Holidays and Special Occasions

Holidays are times when families and friends gather together to celebrate and share memories of years past. Most often older adults want to be included in the family gatherings, but you may need to modify the plans to accommodate their limitations. Extending a holiday invitation to older adults will make them feel like an important part of the celebration.

Birthdays

◆ Celebrate an older loved one's birthday with a gift of memories that she will cherish. If the honoree is turning eighty-four, compile a list of eighty-four special memories about the older adult. Ask family members and friends to contribute their memories in advance of the celebration. Either frame the list or place it in an

Tips for making holidays more enjoyable

Stand in their orthopedic shoes. Be sensitive to the changes in an older adult's life. A loss of strength and stamina may make traditional get-togethers increasingly difficult. Be prepared to adjust the time that your older loved one stays at an event. Think about ramps needed to accommodate walkers and wheelchairs.

Control environment. Older adults with hearing or vision impairments are especially vulnerable to sensory overload. Being in the midst of a crowd of people can make them nervous or irritable. Make family members aware of how noise or excessive activity can affect an older loved one and make appropriate accommodations.

Don't think of elders as children. Remember that older adults are not children, even if their needs have

album. The older adult will take pleasure in reading and rereading the memories that total her age.

◆ If the older person is a fan of crossword puzzles, have a one-of-a-kind crossword puzzle made about the life of the honoree. You can find puzzle-making services online. Use interesting trivia about her life: her nickname, the place she was born, the name of her first pet, etc.

changed dramatically. Always treat them with dignity and respect.

Allow them time to grieve. For some older adults, the thought of a holiday spent without a beloved spouse is overwhelming. Don't try to force your good cheer upon an older loved one who is in the midst of grief. Usually it is best just to be at their side and offer support.

Involve them in preparations. Many older adults want to be included in the preparations for holiday festivities even though their tasks may need to be modified. Think about tasks your older loved one can do comfortably. A grandmother might make the place cards for the table. A grandfather could write a prayer to say before dinner. Ask older loved ones how they would like to be involved.

Anniversaries

◆ Mark a milestone wedding anniversary with a reception that highlights the year the couple married. Search online or in the library for a copy of a local newspaper published on the day that the couple was married. Note the stories of the day. Incorporate the headlines and advertisements into the decorations or use as an invitation. Utilize any memorabilia from their wedding day. Ask members of a Bible study class or small group to send cards to your older loved ones for their anniversary celebration. They will be thrilled to have a mailbox stuffed with good wishes.

◆ Turn an anniversary celebration into a mission effort. Ask family members and friends to match the number of years a couple has been married with the number of items donated to a food pantry in honor of the older couple. For example, if they have been married sixty years, a family might donate sixty cans of soup or sixty boxes of pasta.

Valentine's Day

◆ Valentine's Day is not just for young romantics. It's an opportunity to remember older loved ones who may still be grieving the loss of a spouse. For a lonely widow, consider hosting an afternoon tea for two. Bring everything you need to host a private celebration. From tea cups and background music to scones and tea sandwiches, pack it all up in a basket and take it to her residence. She will appreciate a private party with you. For the widower, substitute a manly Valentine's Day breakfast. He too will appreciate your efforts to share your love on this special day.

Lent and Easter

◆ During the season of Lent, ask older adults to write a daily blessing on a slip of paper and drop it into their own Blessing Box. On Easter Sunday, invite them to open their boxes and reread the blessings so they can see how God has been at work in their lives.

◆ Host an ecumenical Good Friday Tenebrae service at a senior residence. Or adapt a Stations of the Cross experience in which older adults can move at their own pace to different areas of a room and read scripture and pick up physical reminders of Christ's journey to the cross.

Mother's Day, Father's Day

◆ Treat your older loved one like a queen on Mother's Day. Honor her with an intimate garden party. Set up a table outside where she can enjoy blooming plants of the season. If you have access to her heirloom dishes, use them as a special tribute. Place photos that showcase her as a mother or grandmother on the table. Ask her children and grandchildren to share special memories.

◆ Host a Father's Day luncheon in honor of your aging father, grandfather, or great-grandfather. Draw inspiration from his interests and hobbies. For example, if he was a fisherman, use a minnow bucket to hold fresh flowers or grasses. Incorporate a tackle box, a stringer and hookless lures into the tabletop decorations. Display a photo of him on a past fishing trip. Paying homage to his special interests will bring him great joy.

Patriotic holidays

◆ For many older adults, nothing says Fourth of July like an old-fashioned neighborhood parade. When possible, give your loved one a front-row seat to watch a local parade. If he doesn't mind staying up late, invite him to watch the fireworks show too. Provide him with a small flag and a patriotic T-shirt. If your loved one is a veteran, honor him for service to his country.

◆ Ask an older adult about his memories of past summer celebrations and he will likely mention ice cream. Let your loved one know that you will be bringing a freezer of homemade ice cream for him to share with his neighbors and friends on a holiday afternoon. Take disposable bowls, spoons, and star-studded napkins too. Offer to help dip the ice cream and clean up.

Halloween or fall festival

◆ Encourage an older adult to participate in a costume party at her retirement community or church. If she seems overwhelmed by the idea of putting a costume together, offer to do it for her. Inexpensive jogging suits provide the foundation for many costumes. Add stripes or spots of iron-on felt for an easy animal get-up. If she uses a walker or power chair, decorate it too; but keep safety a priority. Bottom line: Do all you can to help an older adult have fun!

◆ Invite an older loved one to hand out candy to the trick-or-treaters at your home. Sit with him on the front porch so that he doesn't have to get up and down every time the doorbell rings. Or check with his church to see if they are hosting a fall festival where the children come in costume. Either way, he will enjoy interacting with the children.

Thanksgiving

◆ Before the family's Thanksgiving dinner, go around the table and have family members give a reason why they are especially thankful for their older loved one. An aging grandfather will be touched to hear the grandchildren tell how they remember the way he fixed their bicycles and taught them to build a campfire. Forget the turkey; pass the tissues.

◆ Do you have a photo of your older loved one from a past Thanksgiving? Perhaps she is carving the turkey or baking the pumpkin pie. Resize and duplicate the photo to make place cards for your Thanksgiving table. She will be honored to discover her picture at each place setting.

Christmas

◆ Decorate a small tree with mementos and trinkets that belong to an aging loved one. Look around for small items like travel souvenirs, costume jewelry, or school memorabilia. Display the tree on a table for a family celebration. Or deck the boughs of a small tree with photos from your loved one's life. Sort through her stash of old photographs for images from her youth. When necessary, scan and reduce the size of the photos. Prop the photos in the tree as personalized ornaments that will have everyone talking long after Christmas is past.

◆ For an older adult confined to a bed or recliner, display a Christmas tree outside the window of her bedroom. Decorate the tree with lights, using a timer so the lights will automatically go on and off. As darkness comes, her mood will be lifted when the lights on the tree begin to twinkle.

New Year's

◆ Your older loved one may find it difficult to stay awake until midnight on New Year's Eve. Suggest that she and her friends celebrate with the people in an earlier time zone. Help them to learn about the traditions and culture of Australia, Africa, Europe, or South America. Assist with appropriate decorations and food to make their New Year's celebration unique!

◆ A new year, a new calendar. Give an older loved one a wall calendar personalized with family photos. These are widely available. Make sure that the birthdays, anniversaries, and other special days of the family are posted on the correct dates.

Gift ideas

◆ Most older adults don't have space for another gadget or gizmo. However, an older loved one would likely appreciate a gift card for the pharmacy where she gets her prescriptions filled or for the hair salon, grocery store, housecleaning service, or dog groomer.

◆ Make a donation to the music department of a loved one's church. Ask that an anthem be purchased in his honor. Find out when the choir will be performing the anthem, and make every effort to take him to hear it.

◆ Give an older loved one a variety of cards—birthday, sympathy, get well, thinking of you—and a roll of stamps so that she can send cards to others.

◆ Older adults will appreciate a space-saving digital photo frame that rotates a series of pictures. Many digital frames have enough memory to store hundreds of photos. Present the digital frame with the photos already loaded. Your loved one will be surprised by the continuing revolution of images.

Bridging the Generation Gap

In a world often segregated by age, it is important to find ways to bring the generations together. Take initiative—intentionally plan activities that build relationships between young and old.

◆ **Family trivia.** Ask an older loved one to help create a family trivia test to share at the next family reunion. Include questions about the various generations, including those members who have passed away.

Who was president of his or her high school senior class?
Who once fell out of an oak tree and broke both arms?
Name three family members who share a middle name.

Give the test to family members. Even amid the competition, they will be building a bond. Invite the older person to read the answers and give a prize to the winner.

◆ **Multigenerational Bible study.** Bringing the generations together to study scripture is a powerful way to break down barriers between age groups. Younger participants will be blessed by interacting with older adults who have gained wisdom that comes with long life. They will also be inspired by their older classmates who are still learning and growing. The older adults will enjoy the energy and fresh thoughts of the younger generations.

◆ **Senior prom.** Ask a church youth group to host a "senior" prom at the church or at a retirement community. Many older adults will be delighted to put on their dancing shoes and take a spin with a young man or woman. Even those in wheelchairs can be pushed and gently twirled. It is an opportunity for teenagers to serve senior adults with physical limitations. It will also help them overcome their fear of the aged. Make it a festive occasion with decorations and refreshments. Select music from the days when the older adults were young.

◆ **Pay it forward.** Think about skills that older adults might teach younger people. Does an older loved one crochet or knit? Does he play chess? Match a young person with an older adult who has a skill to pass along. Provide them with the supplies they need.

◆ **Computer buddies.** Many older adults are intimidated by fast-changing technology. Their younger counterparts have an opportunity to minister to seniors by showing them how to use computers and other technologies to connect with family and friends. Some older adults may only be interested in setting up an e-mail account. Others may be interested in learning social networking or how to surf the internet for items of interest. Ask for volunteers who are willing to teach an older adult basic technology information in a one-on-one setting.

◆ **Grandchild star.** Help an older adult feel a part of a family event, even when he cannot attend. Record a grandchild or great-grandchild in a school performance or sporting event. Play the video for your older loved one and have the child describe his participation.

◆ **Send a postcard.** On family vacations, encourage young family members to mail postcards to their aging grandparents and great-grandparents. Ask each child to tell about the sights and activities of the day. The older adult will be excited to receive updates about the trip.

◆ **Let the children come.** Nothing breathes fresh air into the life of an older adult like an infant or a toddler. Ask family members or friends with young children to visit an aging loved one with their little one in tow. Encourage the young parent to ask the older adult for words of wisdom about raising children.

◆ **Signs of surprise.** Brighten the day of older adults who live alone or who spend most of their time inside by surprising them with personalized yard signs. Ask youth and children to create festive signs with large-print messages of affection and encouragement like "Have a blessed day!" Shop for blank yard signs at office supply retailers and online stores or use poster board to create your own. Decorate both sides so that the signs can be visible to the senior adult and also to passersby. Quietly plant the signs in the early morning hours if possible. The older adults will be surprised when the sun comes up on their sea of good wishes.

Building a Legacy

A meaningful legacy is not about money or personal belongings. It involves influence that ripples into the future. Help older adults think about the legacy they want to leave behind.

◆ **Journaling with purpose.** Encourage an older loved one to create a journal for each of her grandchildren or great-grandchildren. Provide her with blank journals and colorful pens. Remind her that journals are ongoing projects not intended to be finished in a short time span. Writing personal notes and reflections for each child will give an older adult a sense of purpose.

◆ **Bringing the family reunion to her.** If your aging loved one is unable to travel to a family reunion, bring the family reunion to her. Treat her to a personalized family T-shirt. Videotape family members speaking directly to her, sharing their favorite memories. For example:

Aunt Sue, I remember when I was young and visited your house each summer. You always made my favorite sugar cookies. From the moment I walked in the door, you made me feel so special. Thank you!

- **Words of wisdom paper weight.** Invite your older loved one to write words of wisdom he'd most like his family members to embrace. Encourage him to limit it to a sentence or two. Reduce the size of the handwritten note and make a copy for every family member. Place each note inside a glass paperweight for family members to keep at their desks. The paperweights will serve as a visual reminder of their older loved one's legacy. You can find paperweights online and in many craft stores.

- **Video storybook.** Older adults have a wealth of stories from their long lives that can benefit younger generations. Create a video storybook of an aging loved one's life. Using a digital recorder, smart phone, or tablet to capture the video, ask the older adult questions. You might use the questions in the first chapter of this book as inspiration. Ask the older adult to tell the stories that are most important to him. Share the video with family and friends for years to come.

- **Bible legacy.** Contact family members about purchasing a Bible for every grandchild or great-grandchild of an older loved one. Ask the older person to mark her favorite scriptures and to write personal notes in the margin. The Bibles will be a treasured gift.

◆ **Writing a memoir.** Every older adult has a story to tell but few believe they could ever write it. In fact, many seniors consider the idea of writing a memoir for their family and friends daunting. It is important to let your loved one know that you will be tackling the big writing project in tiny bites. Begin by introducing a specific topic or use one of the questions in the first chapter of this book. Reassure her that following a chronological timeline is not necessary. Give your older adult questions and other topics to work on for half an hour each day. As she continues the writing journey, ask her to gather photographs that correspond to her stories. Use the computer to scan and assemble the photos and text into a treasured memoir.